Manifestations Now Affirmations

ISBN:9780989067324

Editing: Alesha Brown at AleshaBrown.net.

Interior Design & Published by:

Sunday Publishing at
www.SundayPublishingCompany.com

Table of Contents

Introduction

Excerpt from *Manifestations Now! Believe, Trust & Walk out your Destiny*:

"I gained joy through journaling, which helped relieve my pain from my brother's passing and losing my job twice. Journaling allowed me to express my thoughts, dreams and cares in writing. Before I realized what I was truly doing, I had penned a vast amount of gems about life. My journals transformed into a book entitled Sunday Grief, M.D., *which helps others throughout the world when difficult situations arise in their lives."*

--Dr. Renee Sunday

Well, there you have it: journaling literally chronicled the worse moments of my life and created a platform for the doors that God was opening. I want you to have the same experience.

This book was written as a companion to, *Manifestations Now! Believe, Trust & Walk out your Destiny*. (Now available at www.ReneeSunday.com and at most major online retailers.)

In the journey of life, we often feel helpless and hopeless. Uncertainty about our future, current events and life in general, often leave us in a state of chaos, confusion and depression. During these times, we need a sign – a manifestation.

We need a glimmer of hope, an indication of greatness or a promise; anything that points to a time where things will be better than they are now.

In order for you to have *Manifestations NOW* and *Believe, Trust & Walk out your Destiny*, you must thoroughly analysis your present for a roadmap to your future. Walk with me, through the tools found in this companion journal, and begin your journey to YOUR destiny and expected end.

--Dr. Renee Sunday

Manifestations Occurring Every Second of the Day

Did you know that manifestations occur **EVERY SECOND of each day**? Did you know that there are two ways in which you can manifest the results you want out of life?

Way #1 – do nothing. You can simply do nothing, wait and hope that the things you desire out of life, arrive by pure happenstance.

Way #2 - work diligently, each and every day, to bring your desired results closer to you.

Bottom line: I want you to receive results! I am passionate about your success: I know, firsthand, that manifestations occur every second of the day. I learned, the hard way, that manifesting our desires into our every day reality is a process we can master. Don't be deceived; often our manifestations appear as vague thoughts that we must nurture to maturity.

Just like *faith without works is dead,* knowledge by itself, is useless. I am a medical doctor, but the degree by itself, does not make a difference in the lives of my patients. Only when knowledge, intent, desire and action are combined, will things really start to happen. This will be the beginning of your pathway to manifestations.

Let me provide another illustration. You might possess the knowledge on how to grow a garden. However, that sheer knowledge will not motivate you to continually water, till the ground or pull up the weeds, especially in the heat of the day. Only when you see yourself picking ripe fresh tomatoes and enjoying them so much, will the desire move you to action.

The desire to fulfill your vision propels you to act: buy, plant and water the seeds. Once this process is complete, the vegetable garden can become a reality.

Similarly, there is a roadmap available, RIGHT NOW, for manifesting your dream life. Here's the step-by-step process revealed for you:

Determine the Idea

Ask yourself, *in an ideal world, what would be different about my current situation? If I could have absolutely any outcome I wanted for this particular problem, what would that look like?* Be very specific and don't get bogged down with what appears to be impossible.

Brainstorm at least three different answers. If you catch that little voice in the back of your head saying, *no, that's not possible*, ignore it. Don't stop the journey.

1) _____

_____

_____

2) _____

_____

_____

3) _____

_____

_____

Virtualize the Idea

Close your eyes and imagine that "it" exist right now: that "it" does happen and "it" has already happened. Feel grateful that the ideal did happen; understand how it changes your life.

Of course, you know that your ideal scenario will be a process and you have to Believe, Trust and Walk out your journey. God has put your purpose in you and, in the right season, people will manifest in your life to bring all things to fruition.

Realize the Idea

As your virtual life gets very close to your "real" life, you will feel it so powerful that you have no choice but to speak about it as truth. You will have no choice but to take actions toward your "virtual" life that will manifest it into your reality. You start to look forward to look forward to it so much that the joy of having your "virtual" life, soaks right through you.

Manifest the Idea

Many people are so frustrated and upset about not having what they want that they focus on their lack. This, of course, creates the complete opposite result desired.

Affirmations are powerful visualization and speaking tools that can be used to imprint your subconscious. This will empower you and imprint on your mind, God's promises for your life.

Be sure to catch your mind when it veers off course to concentrate on the wrong things. Pull it back into submission by concentrating on the right things. To illustrate, always believe that:

- You have a right to have what you want.

- You are personally worthy of anything you want.

- The world has plenty of whatever you want to go around.

- There is a higher purpose in having what you want.

- Having what you want is attainable.

- You are already grateful for your future abundance.

- Negative thoughts never serve you.

Master the 4-step manifestation process, keep your thoughts focused on what is positive and productive, and you will be surprised how quickly you can manifest your dream life.

The following *Manifestations Affirmations* will be a daily guide for you to embrace and experience results in your life, every second of the day.

You have a calling, a purpose and a destiny for your life. Believe, Trust and Walk Out Your Destiny. Manifestations Are Now!!!

MANIFESTATIONS NOW!!!!

What Manifestations do you desire?

Manifestations Now! Believe, Trust & Walk out your Destiny, shared compelling testimonies of the lives of a few believers. You will have what you believe: what do you believe God for?

The following self-analysis is vital: you must first discover the heart of your beliefs before you can manifest those things you desire in life. What you believe is what you have; what you speak, is what you will receive.

Self-Check:

Q: Are you able to discern illusions and appearances from reality?

A: _____

_____

_____

Q: Do you believe that there are limitless, overflowing blessings stored up for you? Why or why not?

A: _____

_____

_____

Q: Do you worry a lot, suffer from anxiety or unrest about what your future holds? Do you sometimes feel like the life of your dreams will never be more than just a dream?

A: _____

_____

_____

Self-Check (continued):

Q: Do you ever feel that you are not "enough"?
(I.e., not smart enough, rich enough, successful
enough, thin enough, strong enough or just
somehow, *not enough*?)

A: _____

_____

_____

Q: Are you open to possibilities? Is your mind, body
and spirit, in a place to receive those things that you
really want?

*(You will have what you believe. You will
prepare to receive.)*

A: _____

_____

_____

Q: Do you believe that you were made in God's image?
How so?

A: _____

_____

_____

Self-Check (continued):

Q: Do you feel that you do not have the life you want
because you are a victim of circumstance? Do you
feel that you are simply in the *wrong place at the
wrong time?*

A: _____

_____

_____

Q: Do you trust God with your WHOLE life? Do you
trust He will work it out in EVERY area of your life?

A: _____

_____

_____

Q: When you are at a crossroads in your life, what is
the FIRST thing you do? Call someone, worry and
fuss or go to God in prayer? *(Be honest.)*

A: _____

_____

_____

Self-Check (continued):

Q: Do you read your bible every day? Do you study it daily? (There is a difference between *reading* and *studying*.)

A: _____

_____

_____

Q: Can you name at least three things that you feel are impossible, or you can't imagine yourself a part of, in your life?

A: _____

_____

_____

Q: How would you describe your average day? If your life was a reality TV show, what would the title be?

A: _____

_____

_____

Self-Check (continued):

Q: Do you find it easy to start working on something, or believing in something, but have a habit of never finishing what you start?

A: _____

_____

_____

Q: Do you often feel alone and abandoned? Do you feel like you're in an uphill battle with yourself?

A: _____

_____

_____

Q: Do you have trust issues? (Trusting others, trusting that life will work in your favor or trusting that you are capable of handling the life you dreamed?)

A: _____

_____

_____

Self-Check (continued):

Q: Are you in "perfect peace" or are you often anxious, too busy or consumed with the pressures of life?

A: _____

_____

_____

Q: Do you have relationships that are healthy? Are you the giver, 9 times out of 10, or do you receive equal or more than you give?

A: _____

_____

_____

Q: Do you often feel misunderstood or not heard?

A: _____

_____

_____

Self-Check (continued):

Q: What are the top things that you are concerned about (that you think about the most)? What are your first thoughts when you go to bed and when you wake up in the morning?

A: _____

_____

_____

Q: What major defeat or failures have you experienced in life? Which replays in your mind and spirt?

A: _____

_____

_____

Q: What is God's purpose for your life? What are your plans for achieving that?

A: _____

_____

_____

Self-Check (continued):

Q: What legacy will you leave on this world? What legacy would you leave if you died right now?

A: _____

_____

_____

Q: Are you a poor "steward"? In what ways do you waste resources that are given to you?

A: _____

_____

_____

Q: Do you believe that YOU were born to succeed?

A: _____

_____

_____

MANIFESTATIONS AFFIRMATIONS

Now that you have taken an honest assessment of your life, take a moment to reflect on what you have learned. Some areas might have really challenged you, and that's okay. The difficult areas identify those things that block you from having the life you want. Make sure you pray over them daily, just as you should with the affirmations.

This step is so vital and often overlooked with books and programs that push affirmations. Just the act of repeating words will not produce results. You must first believe before you decree. Remember, according to the word, whenever you decree a thing, it will be done. *Choose your words, and the spirit in which you release them, WISELY.*

Now that you have done your beginning the work, you have the right context and platform to recite the following affirmations. Repeat them a minimum of three times a day. You might want to implement a dedicated time every day.

Any affirmations that you struggle with, go back to your above questions and answers, and pray to the Lord for guidance on how to deal with these areas.

Affirmations to Manifest What You Want Out of Life:

- ➢ I see right through appearances and illusions and know that my manifestations will come to fruition.

- ➢ The manifestation of my thoughts and actions, is the compass for God's perfect direction for my desires.

- ➢ I am thankful for the limitless, overflowing Source of my manifestations now.

- ➢ I am showered with blessings and my Divine Inheritance.

- ➢ God provides me with all that I desire, whenever I desire it, for as long as I desire it.

- ➢ God provides me with more than enough substance and supply.

- ➢ I am readily, openly and freely accepting my manifestations now!

- ➢ I receive an unmatchable supply of manifestations for my Life daily.

- ➢ I am always in the right place at the right time.

- ➢ I live in the likeness and image of God's Divine Manifestations.

- ➢ For the joy of the LORD is my strength.

Affirmations to Manifest What You
Want Out of Life (continued):

➤ This is the day which the LORD has made; I will rejoice and be glad in it.

➤ I trust in the Lord with all my heart, and lean not unto my own understanding. In all my ways I acknowledge Him and He shall direct my paths.

➤ Jesus keeps me in perfect peace, as my mind is stayed on Him, because I trust in Him.

➤ I wait upon the Lord, and He renews my strength. I mount up with wings as eagles, I run and am not weary. I walk, and am not faint.

➤ My delight is in the law of the Lord and in His law do I meditate day and night. I shall be like a tree planted by the rivers of water, that brings forth his fruit in his season. My leaf also shall not wither; whatever I do, shall prosper.

➤ My God shall supply all my needs according to His riches in glory, by Christ Jesus.

➤ God is able to do exceeding, abundantly, above all that I ask or think, according to His power that works in me.

➤ I keep the words of God's covenant, and do them, that I may prosper in all that I do.

➤ With God, all things are possible.

Affirmations to Manifest What You
Want Out of Life (continued):

- ➤ I can do all things through Christ, which strengtheneth me.

- ➤ I seek first the Kingdom of God, and His righteousness, and all these things shall be added unto me.

- ➤ I welcome positive energy and I use that feeling to accomplish more.

- ➤ I use my energy to live my life to the fullest.

- ➤ No matter what I'm working on, I'm always committed to completing my goal.

- ➤ I trust my thought processes; they are clear and I am very capable.

- ➤ I have love, peace, joy and success with God.

- ➤ God will NEVER leave or forsake me.

- ➤ My life is protected from hurt, harm or danger.

- ➤ No matter how hard I may fall, I get back up, dust myself off and forge on.

- ➤ No matter the challenge, God will strengthen me to go through it.

- ➤ I enjoy being responsible for my actions.

Affirmations to Manifest What You
Want Out of Life (continued):

- ➢ My life is full of purpose, exciting change and many recognized deeds.

- ➢ By commemorating the smallest nuggets of success, I am motivated to complete the larger tasks.

- ➢ I enjoy connecting with others.

- ➢ I am grateful for the opportunity to connect with others.

- ➢ I contribute to the healthy development of my relationships.

- ➢ My relationship is leading to love and commitment.

- ➢ All of my relationships are positive, loving and productive.

- ➢ All of my relationships are honest, loyal and trusting.

- ➢ I'm in a fulfilling and nurturing relationship.

- ➢ My ability to communicate is enhanced with my power to listen.

- ➢ When I speak with other people, our conversation involves giving and receiving.

- ➢ My body language makes me approachable to everybody.

Affirmations to Manifest What You
Want Out of Life (continued):

- ➤ I speak the reality with sincerity, knowledge and compassion.

- ➤ I'm an excellent, compassionate and loving to everyone I meet.

- ➤ My ability to communicate draws other people closer to me.

- ➤ The one that I truly adore returns to me with open arms of love.

- ➤ It's simple for me to express love and in return, it's easily expressed back to me.

- ➤ I'm open to experiencing bonding on different levels with others that I meet.

- ➤ I show love to others through my gratitude and positive interaction.

- ➤ I'm ready to connect with others in a godly and purposeful way.

- ➤ I'm successful in everything I do.

- ➤ I joyfully receive wealth and abundance in my life.

- ➤ Money comes to me often and easily to advance His Kingdom.

Affirmations to Manifest What You
Want Out of Life (continued):

- It's great to have money! I'm ready for Manifestations Now!

- I handle all of my finances wisely.

- I am successful in everything I execute.

- I am a willing vessel for God's Glory.

- I'll reach my goals, joyfully and easily.

- I invest wisely.

- I am always accomplishing my goals, in a spirit of excellence.

- I joyfully receive wealth and abundance in my life.

- It is great to have an income!

- I love being one of God's Ambassadors.

- I'm so happy to be a part of God's Plan.

- I am creating wealth to leave a legacy to my children's children.

- Every day, and in every way, I am getting better and better being a steward of my money.

Affirmations to Manifest What You
Want Out of Life (continued):

➢ I am thankful that my life has purpose and meaning. I am unique and special. There is nobody on earth exactly like me.

➢ I am chosen, confident and compassionate.

➢ I was created in the image of God. I am wonderfully made.

➢ I was born to succeed.

➢ I am loved by God and He first loved me.

➢ I am thankful that my life is filled with God's Favor.

➢ I will speak God's Word.

➢ I Believe, Trust and Walk out My DESTINY.

➢ I thank God for His Grace and Mercy.

Get Purpose Now!

Everyone has a calling. Let Dr. Sunday help you discover your purpose.

Renee Sunday, M.D., is the Founder and CEO of Sunday Publishing Company, LLC, and RS Commerce, P.C.

She is on a mission to encourage and empower others to enjoy life and obtain their dreams. Practicing anesthesia for over thirteen years, she enjoys being an instrument in God's Plan to render services and show compassion, love and the "standard of care". Every day she empowers others to propel their message to the world.

Renee is a radio and television personality:

- Host of Good Deeds Radio & TV Show
- Platform Builder
- Grief & Loss Specialist
- Group Counselor
- Motivational & Inspirational Coach
- Passion & Purpose Guru
- Author
- Publisher
- Anesthesiologist

Renee's passion is to be a catalyst to stimulate others toward their destiny. She experienced this, firsthand, when she went from 6 figures to 0 in 24 hours. For fourteen years, she thought her purpose was serving as an anesthesiologist. When one door closed, several new doors opened and continue to do so, as of this day.

Everyone has a purpose. Everyone has a calling. Everyone has reason to be on the earth right now. A lot of people are asking, "Why was I created?" They want to know God's grand purpose for their life.

The truth of the matter is many people are not called to one sole area or thing. There are many things we enjoy in life. Can you say you are enjoying life? If you are frustrated with your job, career or life in general, there is help for where you are right now.

Get Purpose Now with Dr. Renee Sunday: she will encourage, empower and equip you to propel your passions to purpose. One step will lead to an abundant supply of opportunities, fulfillment of dreams and achieving a purpose driven life.

The Sunday Foundation – The Founder:

The Sunday Foundation (SF) is a 501(c)(3) nonprofit organization. SF is a foundation of action, which propels individuals into their purpose in life.

The Sunday Foundation creates, finds and supports individuals who want to improve their thinking and well-being. SF offers opportunities that will empower individuals to obtain a fulfilled, joyful and thriving life.

SF's Visionary and Founder, Dr. Renee Sunday, states: "I have practiced anesthesia for over thirteen years. My mission is to encourage and empower others to enjoy life, share their message and obtain their dreams. Furthermore, I enjoy being an instrument to render services to others and show compassion, love and the standard of care".

Dr. Sunday experienced loss of both her brother William Sunday, Jr. and Godson - Eyianlijah. During the time at the hospitals, especially while in the intensive care unit (ICU), she noticed supportive families were tired and physically exhausted. Many of the families were in need of basic necessities and support for themselves. Sunday Foundation (SF) was birthed to be a part of the solution to satisfy the needs of families and continue to serve as one of the extended family members.

Our Mission

Our Mission is serving individuals to embark and obtain their purpose throughout communities near and far. Opportunities are few and far between - SF is here to bridge the gap with programs, necessities and resources, tailored to serve and meet the needs of each individual.

We will accomplish the mission through programs, seminars, workshops, awards, recognition and other benchmarked resources designed to propel individuals in life. For more information, please visit:

www.TheSundayFoundation.org

Manifestations Now Affirmations. Sunday Publishing Company.

www.ingramcontent.com/pod-product-compliance
Lightning Source LLC
Chambersburg PA
CBHW071458070426
42452CB00040B/1877